CHOCOLATE HEAVEN

The All-Chocolate Cookbook

by Lisa deMauro
illustrated by Jeanie Friedman

Parachute Press, Inc.

Parachute Press, Inc.
200 Fifth Avenue, Rm. 461
New York, New York 10010

Copyright © 1987 by Parachute Press, Inc.
ISBN: 0-938753-08-8

First printing 1987
Printed in the U.S.A.

Typeset by Contour Type, Inc.
Design by Michel Design

Contents

1 BASICS

This is a cookbook for chocolate lovers. You know who you are. You don't simply *like* chocolate. You *love* it. And you want to cook with it and bake with it and make drinks with it and give parties with it. If you want to do all that, this cookbook will show you how.

But before you begin, read through this first chapter. It tells you about working with chocolate. And it gives some ground rules so you can make masterpieces in the kitchen and still keep peace in the family.

RULES OF THE KITCHEN

1. Always ask a parent for permission to use the kitchen. Follow the rules of your household. Many parents insist that kids cook only when an adult is present. And check to make sure you are free to use the ingredients you will need. (You don't want to use the last egg just as your mom or dad is about to make an omelet for lunch.)

2. Wash your hands, *often*. Start any cooking project with clean hands. Wash them whenever you get them covered with food. (You don't want to leave a sticky trail of brownie batter or marshmallow creme all over the place.)

3. Be careful. Use potholders to hold pans on the stove or to take pans out of the oven. (Never use a wet potholder!) Don't balance a bowl of boiling water on the edge of a counter. Keep the dog out of your way. *Concentrate* on what you are doing.

4. Read through a recipe before you begin cooking. Make sure you understand what you have to do. If you don't understand the steps in a recipe, ask an adult to help you figure them out. Make sure you have all the equipment and ingredients you need. (You don't want to get halfway through a recipe and *then* find out you need an ostrich feather.)

5. Prepare the kitchen. Will you need a large counter space? Will you need room in the refrigerator or freezer? It's better to get things ready *before* you begin. Then you can go full speed ahead.

6. Clean up along the way. Put dirty bowls and spoons in the sink or dishwasher when you are through with them. If you have a few minutes between steps, wipe up spills and put away ingredients you no longer need. When you are finished, *do a very good job of cleaning up the kitchen.* (If you don't, you may never get a chance to cook again!)

MELTING CHOCOLATE

When you cook with chocolate, the melting can be tricky. Chocolate burns when it gets too hot. So, if possible, keep it away from direct contact with the stove.

TO MELT CHOCOLATE: Use a bowl that is large enough to hold the chocolate without piling it up too much. If you're melting chocolate chips, you should be able to spread them out so that they aren't more than 4 or 5 deep. If you're melting baking chocolate, every square should be against the bottom of the bowl. They shouldn't be stacked up 2 or 3 squares high.

A metal bowl is best for melting chocolate. Glass is okay, too. Plastic and pottery bowls don't absorb heat as well, so it may take longer to melt chocolate in them.

Make sure the bowl is absolutely dry. Put the baking chocolate or chocolate chips in the bowl. You'll also need another bowl, larger than the one with the chocolate in it. It should be big enough so that there is at least an inch of space around the smaller bowl when it sits in the bigger one.

Fill a saucepan or a kettle with 3 or 4 cups of water and set the pan on the stove over medium heat until the water boils. (If you cover the pan, it will boil more quickly.) Use a potholder to take the pan from the heat.

Carefully pour about a cup of water into the larger bowl. Gently put the smaller bowl inside the larger one. Be very careful

6

not to let *any* water or steam get into the bowl with the chocolate. The level of the water around the outside of the smaller bowl should be at least as high as the level of the chocolate *inside* the bowl. If it's not high enough, take the smaller bowl out. Add more water to the larger bowl and then put the smaller bowl back. The heat of the water against the bowl will melt the chocolate. Stir the chocolate from time to time. If the water cools before the chocolate is melted, change the cool water for more hot water.

SPECIAL NOTE: If you have a double boiler and know how to use it, you can melt the chocolate in the top of a double boiler. Make sure it is dry. Put the pan over, but not sitting in, hot water. Don't let the water boil. It's important to keep the temperature down and not to allow steam to get into the chocolate.

A Problem Solver

If even a tiny bit of water or steam gets into melted chocolate, it becomes thick and pasty. To make the chocolate soften and become liquid again, stir in a teaspoon of vegetable oil (not olive oil). If the chocolate is still thick, add a bit more oil.

THE CHOCOLATE CHIP CODE

What do the chocolate chips at the beginning of each recipe mean?

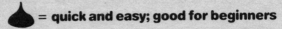 = quick and easy; good for beginners

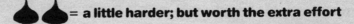 = a little harder; but worth the extra effort

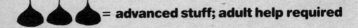 = advanced stuff; adult help required

2 DRINKS

Chocolate may be the most popular drink flavoring on earth. Hot or cold. Mixed with milk, soda, or ice cream. Once upon a time, there *was* no eating chocolate. Food companies didn't make it until the 1800's. People either drank chocolate or did without. Luckily, chocolate comes in many forms today. But when you want a chocolate drink, try one of these.

MEXICAN HOT CHOCOLATE

Chances are, the hot chocolate you've been drinking all these years isn't chocolate at all. It's cocoa. Cocoa is a powder. It's *made* from chocolate, but it isn't chocolate. It isn't thick and smooth like chocolate. It isn't solid. And until it's mixed with milk or water, cocoa is very dry.

In Mexico people drink hot chocolate made from real chocolate, like this.

What You Need

large mixing bowl

wire whisk or eggbeater

kettle or saucepan to boil water

potholder

measuring cups and spoons

mug or cup

½ cup (3 ounces) semisweet chocolate chips

1 cup boiling water

3 tablespoons instant nonfat dry milk powder

dash of almond extract or a shake of ground
   cinnamon

What You Do

1. Measure chocolate chips into bowl.

2. Carefully measure hot water and pour over chocolate chips. Let the chocolate sit for 30 seconds.

3. Add dry milk powder and almond extract or cinnamon.

4. Beat with a wire whisk or eggbeater until all the chocolate is melted and mixture is smooth. Pour into mug or cup and drink.

For two cups, double the ingredients.
For three or four cups, triple or quadruple them.

People in Mexico like hot chocolate so much that they have a special tool just for mixing the chocolate. It's a long, thin stirrer made of carved wood called a *molinillo*. To use it, you put the *molinillo* into the hot chocolate mixture and twirl it back and forth between your palms until the chocolate is frothy.

Montezuma was emperor of the Aztec Indians more than 400 years ago. He was also a world champion chocolate lover. He drank *chocolatl*, a bitter chocolate drink. In fact, he drank over 50 cups a day!

HOT PEPPERMINT COCOA

The next time you lose a snowball fight or get soaked in a nasty drizzle, drink some cocoa. It drives away the chill and will cheer you up. Especially if it's topped with whipped cream, a melting marshmallow, or a scoop of ice cream.

This recipe uses unsweetened cocoa powder. The peppermint hard candy gives you a chocolate mint flavor. If you don't like mint, leave it out.

What You Need

small saucepan

spoon with a plastic handle

potholder

mug or cup

measuring cups and spoons

1 tablespoon cocoa powder

1 tablespoon plus 2 teaspoons sugar

pinch salt

¼ cup water

¾ cup milk

few drops of vanilla extract

1 red-and-white- striped peppermint hard
   candy

What You Do

1. Put cocoa powder, sugar, and salt in saucepan and stir together.

2. Add water slowly and stir until smooth. Turn on heat to low. Use potholder to hold handle of pan.

3. Heat and stir until mixture boils. Keep stirring and boil for two minutes.

4. Add milk slowly, stirring until smooth. Heat until mixture is very hot, but not boiling.

5. Remove from heat.

6. Place peppermint candy in bottom of mug or cup. Pour cocoa over candy.

7. Stir and drink.

Makes one cup. Double or triple the ingredients to make two or three cups.

Parlez-vous Chocolate?

Hot chocolate is a very popular drink in France. Some people drink the hot chocolate out of big bowls and dunk pieces of buttered bread in it. Try it—you'll say it's yummy!

Have you ever heard of a chocolate house? No, it's not a house made out of chocolate. Quit dreaming. It's a place where people could meet and drink hot chocolate. Chocolate houses were very popular in England about 300 years ago. The first one opened in 1657.

SODA-FOUNTAIN DRINKS

There are lots of chocolate soda-fountain drinks—egg creams, sodas, ice cream sodas, and milk shakes. With the ingredients below, you can make fabulous drinks— better than those you get at the local ice-cream parlor.

What You Need

glass

spoon

ice-cream scoop

blender

chocolate syrup

milk

ice cream

club soda or seltzer

CHOCOLATE MILK

There are two ways to make chocolate milk: You can add the chocolate syrup *before* you add the milk or *after*. Use enough syrup to make it as dark and sweet as you like. Stir. Drink. (You can make your own syrup for chocolate milk and other drinks. See the recipe for Heavenly Chocolate Sauce #3 on page 80.)

CHOCOLATE SODA

This is similar to chocolate milk, but a soda uses club soda or seltzer instead of milk. To be authentic, add the syrup first.

CHOCOLATE ICE-CREAM SODA

Make a chocolate soda (with syrup and seltzer). After you stir it up, add a scoop of chocolate ice cream. Drink with a straw. If you want to make a Black and White Soda, use vanilla ice cream instead.

CHOCOLATE EGG CREAM

An egg cream has no egg and no cream. It's really a chocolate soda with a splash of milk. Begin with about two tablespoons of milk. (If you like milk, use more.) Add chocolate syrup and stir. Then add club soda or seltzer and stir again. But don't fill the glass too full. And stir over the sink. Sometimes the fizz heads up and out.

BROWN COW

A Brown Cow is an old-time soda-fountain favorite. It is made with root beer (or sometimes cola), vanilla ice cream, a dash of milk, and chocolate syrup.

HOBOKEN

A Hoboken is made with chocolate ice cream, seltzer, milk, and pineapple syrup. (Pineapple syrup is hard to find, but crushed pineapple is a good substitute.)

CHOCOLATE MILK SHAKE

To make an old-fashioned milk shake, you need a blender. (A milk shake machine is even better.) Put 2 or 3 scoops of chocolate ice cream into the blender container. Add 2 tablespoons of chocolate syrup and a cup of milk. Run the blender on low speed but *not too long*! You don't want the ice cream to turn to liquid. You just want it well mixed.

CHOCOLATE BANANA SMOOTHIE

his drink looks like a health food and tastes like a dessert. It makes a good after-school snack.

What You Need

blender or potato masher and wire whisk

small mixing bowl

mixing spoon

measuring cups and spoons

tall glass

1 ripe banana

½ cup plain or vanilla yogurt

½ cup milk

2 to 4 tablespoons chocolate syr

ice cubes

What You Do

If you're using a blender: Break banana into thirds. Put banana, yogurt, milk, and 2 tablespoons chocolate syrup in container. Cover blender and blend until everything is smooth. If necessary, stop blender once or twice and push down banana pieces with a spoon.

If you're using a potato masher: Put the banana in a bowl. Mash it well with potato masher. (Or use a fork, or just squish it with your fingers, but get it *really* mashed.) Add yogurt, milk, and 2 tablespoons chocolate syrup and blend it all well with a wire whisk.

Whether you use a blender or not: Taste for sweetness and chocolateyness. Add more syrup if you like and blend well. Pour smoothie over ice, and then drink.

Makes one. Double or triple the recipe to make more.

3 NO-BAKE TREATS

You don't need an oven to make these recipes. (For some you do need the top of the stove.) No-bake treats are fun to put together, and they don't take a long time to make. But don't be in too much of a hurry. Some of them take a while to harden or chill.

CREAMY DREAMY MILK CHOCOLATE FUDGE

Making fudge can be tricky. Butter, sugar, chocolate, and milk are heated until they reach just the right temperature. Then the mixture is beaten with a spoon—beaten long enough to make most people's arms tired. This recipe is easier. There's no temperature to take and no beating.

What You Need

large saucepan

rubber spatula

potholder

knife

wooden or plastic-handled spoon

8″ or 9″ square baking pan

wax paper

measuring spoon

1 can (14 ounces) sweetened condensed milk (not evaporated milk)

25 regular-size marshmallows

dash of salt

4 squares (4 ounces) unsweetened baking chocolate, paper wrapper taken off

36 Hershey's Kisses, peeled

1 teaspoon vanilla extract

1 cup chopped nuts (if you like nuts)

What You Do

1. Set out all your ingredients and equipment.

2. Cut a sheet of wax paper that is at least 2 inches larger all around than the pan you are using. Place the wax paper over the inside of the pan and fit it into the pan, creasing the paper at the corners so that it will stay in place. Set the pan aside.

3. Pour the milk into the saucepan. Use a rubber spatula to scrape out the milk that sticks to the side of the can.

4. Add the marshmallows and the dash of salt.

5. Use a potholder to hold the pan. Heat over *very* low heat, stirring often, until marshmallows melt completely.

6. Remove from heat and add baking chocolate.

7. Stir to help chocolate melt evenly. If mixture is too cool to melt chocolate, put pan back over *very* low heat for a few seconds. Keep stirring.

8. When chocolate is melted, add Kisses and stir again to help them melt evenly. If you have to, place pan over *very* low heat again for a few seconds, but be careful not to burn the chocolate. To keep the chocolate from sticking, keep scraping the bottom of the pan with the spatula.

9. When the mixture is very smooth, stir in the vanilla.

10. Add the nuts if you're using them.

11. Spread the fudge in the prepared pan and smooth the top so that it's not too uneven.

12. Refrigerate at least two hours.

13. Cut into squares. Store fudge in a covered container in the refrigerator.

Makes approximately 16 large or 32 small pieces.

CHOCO-PEANUT BUTTER MARBLES

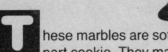

These marbles are soft and chewy. They're part candy, part cookie. They make a fun dessert.

What You Need

small saucepan

potholder

spoon

rubber spatula

mixing bowl

baking sheet

wax paper or aluminum foil

measuring cups and spoons

½ stick (4 tablespoons) margarine

⅓ cup peanut butter, creamy or chunky

2 tablespoons honey

¾ cup (4½ ounces) semisweet chocolate chips

¼ cup instant nonfat dry milk powder

1¼ cups rolled or quick oats (not instant)

What You Do

1. Set out all your ingredients and equipment.

2. Line a baking sheet with wax paper or foil.

3. Put margarine in saucepan over very low heat. When margarine is melted, take off heat.

4. Stir in peanut butter and honey and mix until smooth.

5. Put pan over low heat again and stir until mixture just begins to boil. Bubbles will appear around the edges of the pan.

6. Remove from heat.

7. Add chocolate chips and stir occasionally until they are melted and mixture is smooth.

8. Pour mixture into clean mixing bowl. Use spatula to scrape out pan.

9. Stir in milk powder. Then stir in oats.

10. Wait until mixture is cool enough to handle. Make sure your hands are clean and dry. Take a rounded teaspoonful of the mixture. Roll it between your palms to form it into a ball about the size of a large marble. Place it on the lined baking sheet. Repeat until you use up the mixture. The marbles can be placed close together, but they should not touch.

11. Put baking sheet in refrigerator one hour.

12. Serve or place in a covered container with wax paper between layers and refrigerate.

Makes about 28 marbles.

UPSIDE-DOWN PEANUT BUTTER CUPS

Everyone knows about peanut butter cups—chocolate on the outside, peanut butter inside. These treats are like peanut butter cups turned inside out.

What You Need

mixing bowl

spoon

baking sheet or large plate

measuring cups

plastic wrap

1 cup peanut butter

½ cup honey

1 cup instant nonfat dry milk powder

about 34 Hershey's Kisses, peeled

What You Do

1. Put peanut butter and honey in mixing bowl.

2. Stir together until well mixed.

3. Add milk powder and stir. (This will take some muscle. You might want help.)

22

4. Pinch off pieces of the mixture about the size of a small walnut and roll into balls.

5. Stick point of a Kiss into a ball. Push the Kiss in and pat the peanut butter batter around the Kiss until the chocolate is all covered except for the bottom.

6. Place ball on cookie sheet or large plate with the bottom of the Kiss resting on the plate.

7. Use remaining peanut butter mixture and Kisses.

8. Cover with plastic wrap and refrigerate at least one hour. If you want to store them for a while, put them in a covered container.

Makes about 34.

Where do Hershey's Kisses come from? From Hershey, Pennsylvania, of course. The Hershey company has been making chocolate since 1894. Did you know that in Hershey, Pennsylvania, the street lamps are made in the shape of chocolate kisses? Now, that's a sweet town!

FROSTY BANANA BITES

You can put these mini-banana pops together in a hurry.
But first you have to give the bananas time to freeze.
Put the banana pieces in the freezer at least 30 minutes
or up to 5 hours ahead of time. When you're ready to eat them,
dip them and then freeze them for 3 minutes to let the chocolate
harden. After that they're ready to eat.

What You Need

**mixing bowls and hot water for melting choc-
   olate (see Basics, pages 6–7)**

knife

baking sheet

aluminum foil or wax paper

measuring cups and spoons

toothpicks

bananas

semisweet chocolate chips

vegetable oil

What You Do

1. Set out all your ingredients and equipment.

2. Line baking sheet with foil or wax paper.

3. Cut the bananas into pieces about 1" to 1½" long. (Cut small bananas into 4 pieces; medium bananas into 5 or 6 pieces and large bananas into 7 or 8 pieces.)

4. Set pieces onto lined baking sheet and freeze at least 30 minutes. (If you freeze them longer than 30 minutes, they'll keep getting harder and colder.)

5. Measure out chocolate chips. The amount you need will depend on how many pieces of banana you use. You will need ¼ cup chips and ½ teaspoon vegetable oil for 4 pieces of banana.

6. Melt chocolate over hot water (see Basics, pages 6–7).

7. When chocolate is smooth, stir in oil.

8. Remove bananas from freezer. Put a toothpick into each piece of banana, near the bottom.

9. Dip the banana chunk into the chocolate mixture. (You don't have to coat it completely.)

10. Put the banana on the baking sheet. Return bananas to freezer for 3 minutes. Use toothpicks as handles to remove bananas from tray. Serve immediately.

Don't leave the bananas out of the freezer too long. They'll turn to mush.

QUICKIES

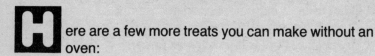ere are a few more treats you can make without an oven:

MARY JANE SUNDAE. Put a scoop of your favorite ice cream on a brownie. Top it with chocolate sauce and whipped cream.

POIRES HÉLÈNE. (That's "Pears Helen" in French.) Put vanilla ice cream in a dish. Top it with a canned pear half (drain it first). Then pour fudge sauce over the pear.

SANDWICH COOKIES. Melt semisweet or milk chocolate chips over hot water (see Basics, pages 6–7). Spread some chocolate on the back of any cookie. (Use vanilla, chocolate, oatmeal, peanut butter, or anything else you like.) Cover the chocolate with another cookie—the same type or a different one. Chill until the chocolate hardens.

FANCY COOKIES. Spread melted semisweet or milk chocolate over the tops of butter or sugar cookies. Dip the chocolate topping in colored sugar, rainbow sprinkles, or chopped nuts. Refrigerate to let the chocolate set.

ICE-CREAM CONE with a chocolate lining. Use melted chocolate and a thin spoon handle or a knife to "paint" the inside of a cone (the hard sugar cone, not the light waffle type of cone). Add a scoop of ice cream or sherbet. Or fill it with peanut butter that is mixed with small banana chunks.

BROWNIES & BAR COOKIES

Every chocolate lover should know how to make brownies. After all: (1) Brownies are quick to make; the batter can be mixed in a saucepan (good for chocolate emergencies). (2) They're neat and easy to carry. (3) And they're very chocolatey.

A special tip: Most recipes call for butter *or* margarine. But for the brownies, butter gives a better texture.

FUDGY BROWNIES

These are the fudgiest! Moist brownies that give you a mouthful of chocolate with every bite. Don't overbake them! They should be soft.

What You Need

medium-size heavy saucepan

large wooden spoon or metal spoon with
   plastic handle

large mixing bowl

measuring cups and spoons

wire whisk or eggbeater

rubber spatula or scraper

aluminum foil, if you want to line the pan
   (See A Baker's Trick, page 30.)

8″ square baking pan

potholder

cooling rack

knife

shortening or vegetable shortening spray to
   grease pan

1 stick (4 ounces) lightly salted butter

2 squares (2 ounces) unsweetened baking
   chocolate, paper wrappers taken off

2 eggs

1 cup sugar

1 teaspoon vanilla extract

½ cup unsifted plain white flour

**½ cup pecans or walnuts broken into pieces
about the size of a pea**

What You Do

1. Set out all your ingredients and equipment.

2. Preheat oven to 325 degrees. (If you use a glass pan, preheat the oven to 300 degrees.)

3. Grease baking pan. (Line it with foil first, if you like.)

4. In a heavy saucepan, melt butter over low heat. Remove
pan from heat.

5. Add chocolate and stir to help chocolate melt evenly.

6. When mixture is smooth, stir in sugar and vanilla extract.

7. Add one egg to mixture and stir well so that you can't see
any egg white or yolk. Then add the second egg and
mix well.

8. Sprinkle flour over the top of batter and stir it in gently.
Be sure that all the flour is blended in, but don't beat the
batter hard.

9. Gently stir in nuts.

10. Pour batter into prepared pan. Use a rubber spatula to scrape out all the batter. Smooth the top and make sure the batter is spread into the corners of the pan.

11. Carefully place pan in preheated oven. Bake for 25 minutes.

12. Use a potholder to remove pan from oven. Place pan on a rack to cool.

13. Refrigerate or freeze before cutting into bars. Brownies will be soft, moist and fudgy. Keep brownies tightly covered and store them in refrigerator or freezer.

Makes approximately 16 large or 32 small brownies.

A Baker's Trick

Here's a trick to make it easy to get your baked brownies out of the pan. Before you add uncooked batter to pan, cut a sheet of aluminum foil large enough to cover the pan with at least an inch extra all around. Turn the pan over so that the back is facing you. Lay the foil across the back of the pan and shape it around the pan. Then turn the pan over and line the inside with foil. Grease the foil with butter, margarine, or vegetable shortening spray.

SPECIAL NOTE: Aluminum foil should not be used in *some* electric ovens. Check with a parent to find out if it's okay to use in your oven.

COCOA BROWNIES

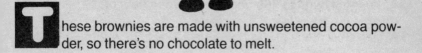

These brownies are made with unsweetened cocoa powder, so there's no chocolate to melt.

What You Need

small mixing bowl

large saucepan

potholder and spoon

measuring cups and spoons

rubber spatula

8" square baking pan

aluminum foil, if you want to line the pan (see
   A Baker's Trick, page 30)

cake tester or toothpick

cooling rack

shortening or vegetable shortening spray to grease pan

⅓ cup unsweetened cocoa powder

1 cup sugar

1 stick plus 2 tablespoons lightly salted butter
   (10 tablespoons in all)

2 eggs

1 teaspoon vanilla extract

½ cup all-purpose flour

½ cup chopped nuts, if you like

What You Do

1. Preheat oven to 350 degrees. (If you use a glass pan, pre-heat the oven to 325 degrees.)

2. Set out all your ingredients and equipment.

3. Lightly grease an 8″ square baking pan. (Line it with foil first, if you like.)

4. Measure cocoa powder and sugar into a small bowl and stir together to blend well and break up any lumps in the cocoa powder.

5. Place butter in saucepan over very low heat. Use a pot-holder to hold the pan by the handle and gently swirl the butter as it melts to keep it from burning. Turn off heat and set pan on a surface that won't burn.

6. Carefully add cocoa-sugar mixture to melted butter. Stir to mix well.

7. Break eggs into small bowl. Use a fork to beat the eggs—just enough to break the yolks and mix them lightly with the whites.

8. Add the eggs to the mixture in the saucepan and stir gently to blend well.

9. Add vanilla extract and stir.

10. Add flour to pan and stir to mix well. Don't leave any lumps of flour.

11. Stir in nuts, if you're using them.

12. Scrape batter into greased baking pan

13. Carefully place pan in preheated oven. Bake about 21-25 minutes. Use cake tester or toothpick to test for doneness. A few crumbs may stick to the tester, but it shouldn't be covered with wet batter.

14. Remove pan to cooling rack. Cool at least 30 minutes before turning out of pan. Or cool completely and cut into bars in pan. Brownies cut best after they are refrigerated. Wrap brownies well and store in refrigerator or freeze.

Makes approximately 16 large or 32 small brownies.

Instead of using nuts in your brownie batter, you might try adding ½ cup of either chocolate chips or dried fruit such as raisins, shredded coconut, or chopped apricots.

CHOCOLATE SYRUP BROWNIES

This is the recipe to use when you're really in a hurry. There's no chocolate to melt and no cocoa to measure. Just take out a jar of chocolate syrup and pour. These brownies come out fudgy and chewy and cakelike. If you want to be scientific, try them at different times using different brands of chocolate syrup.

What You Need

large saucepan

rubber spatula

potholder

8″ square baking pan

aluminum foil, if you want to line the pan (see
A Baker's Trick, page 30)

measuring cups and spoons

cake tester or toothpick

cooling rack

shortening or vegetable shortening spray to
grease pan

1 stick (4 ounces) butter

¾ cup sugar

¾ cup chocolate-flavor syrup

1 egg

1 teaspoon vanilla extract

1 cup flour

What You Do

1. Set out all your ingredients and equipment.

2. Preheat oven to 350 degrees. (If you use a glass pan, pre-heat the oven to 325 degrees.)

3. Line the baking pan with foil if you like, or just grease the pan. Set it aside.

4. Place butter in saucepan and melt it over medium heat.

5. Using potholder to hold handle, swirl the pan to help melt the butter evenly and keep it from burning. Remove the pan from heat.

6. Stir in sugar and blend well.

7. Stir in chocolate-flavor syrup.

8. Add the egg and blend until no white and no yolk is left, but blend gently. Try not to beat air into the batter.

9. Stir in the vanilla extract.

10. Sprinkle the flour in and blend lightly.

11. Spread batter in prepared pan. Use spatula to scrape out pan.

12. Bake in preheated oven 30–35 minutes. Use a cake tester or toothpick to test for doneness. Cool on rack. Cut into bars and serve.

Makes approximately 16 large or 32 small brownies.

CHOCOLATE FUDGE FROSTING

This recipe turns any pan of brownies into a double chocolate treat.

What You Need

medium saucepan

spoon

measuring cups and spoons

½ stick (4 tablespoons) butter or margarine

2 squares (2 ounces) unsweetened chocolate, paper wrappers taken off

2 cups confectioners' sugar

2 tablespoons milk

¼ teaspoon vanilla extract

What You Do

1. Set out all your ingredients and equipment.

2. Put butter or margarine in saucepan and melt over low heat.

3. When shortening is melted, remove from heat.

4. Add unsweetened chocolate. Stir every now and then until chocolate is melted.

5. Add about ½ cup confectioners' sugar and stir to blend well.

6. Add milk and blend well.

7. Add another ½ cup sugar and blend well.

8. Add the remaining sugar. Stir until smooth.

9. Add the vanilla extract.

10. Spread on cooled brownies. Cut and serve.

Makes enough to frost an 8″ or 9″ pan of brownies.

Chocolate lovers, this may surprise you: Almost all the chocolate we buy today has either vanilla extract or artificial vanilla in it. Vanilla, it seems, makes chocolate taste more like chocolate!

Has this ever happened to you? You get a piece of chocolate out of the cupboard, and it's turned all gray and dusty looking. Ugh! Wait! Don't throw it away. There's nothing wrong with it. The dusty stuff is called the bloom. It happens when the cocoa butter in the chocolate comes to the surface. The chocolate may not look beautiful, but it will taste just fine.

PEANUT BUTTER FROSTING

This creamy frosting makes any brownie taste like a peanut butter cup. You can add miniature chocolate chips or chopped peanuts to the frosting or just spread it on in a smooth layer. You can make this frosting without a mixer. But you'll need a strong arm to beat it with a spoon.

What You Need

large mixing bowl

spoon or mixer

butter knife or spatula

measuring cups and spoons

2 tablespoons salted butter or margarine at room temperature

¼ cup smooth peanut butter

1¼ cups confectioners' sugar

3 tablespoons (or more) milk

½ cup miniature chocolate chips or chopped peanuts, if you like

What You Do

1. Set out all your ingredients and equipment.

2. Put the butter or margarine and the peanut butter in a large mixing bowl. Blend them together with a mixing spoon or mixer.

3. Add about half the confectioners' sugar and mix.

4. Add about 2 tablespoons of milk and blend.

5. Add the remaining sugar and blend. Mixture will be thick and hard to mix. You may have to mash the mixture with the back of a spoon, rather than beat it.

6. Add about one more teaspoon of milk and blend.

7. Keep adding more milk, a few drops at a time, and blend well until you have a frosting that is smooth and will spread easily. When the frosting is ready, it should be thick. You will be able to scoop it up with a spoon and then turn the spoon upside down over the bowl and none of the frosting should fall back into the bowl. But if you shake the spoon upside down, the frosting should plop back into the bowl.

8. Stir in chocolate chips or nuts, if you are using them.

9. Spread the frosting onto a pan of cooled brownies and refrigerate at least 30 minutes until the frosting is set.

Makes enough for an 8″ or 9″ pan of brownies.

Chocolate is the perfect melt-in-your mouth food. The reason: cocoa butter. Cocoa butter melts at about 90 degrees Fahrenheit. Want to prove it? Do this serious scientific experiment. Carefully place a piece of chocolate in your mouth. Ummmmm. See, it's melting. Isn't science fun?

BROWNIE TOPPERS

Are you looking for a way to dress up your brownies without taking the time to make a batch of frosting? Here are five quick-fix ideas that are tops.

CHEWY COCO-MALLOW: Mix 1 cup marshmallow creme with ¼ cup flaked coconut. After you put the brownie batter in the pan, top it with heaping teaspoonfuls of the mixture just before you put it in the oven. Bake as usual. Cool, cut, and serve.

MARBLE SWIRL: Sprinkle 1 cup semisweet chocolate chips over the brownie batter just before you put it into the oven to bake. Bake just 2 minutes. Carefully remove the pan from the oven using a potholder. Run the blade of a knife back and forth across the top, cutting about ½" into the batter. The chocolate chips will be melted, and they will swirl into a marble design. Return the pan to the oven and finish baking.

TOASTED MARSHMALLOW: Sprinkle 2 cups of miniature marshmallows over the top of a pan of baked brownies that have just come from the oven. Put the pan back in the oven for about 2 minutes. The marshmallows should begin to turn light brown. Remove from oven. Cool. Then cut and serve.

CHOCOLATE ROOF: As soon as you finish baking a pan of brownies, sprinkle 1 cup of semisweet chocolate chips over the top. Let the pan sit about a minute on a cooling rack. Then smooth out the melted chocolate chips using a knife or spatula. Let the brownies cool about 30 minutes. Use the blade of a knife to draw lines in the chocolate topping where you will cut the brownies into bars. Let the brownies cool completely. Refrigerate until the chocolate is hard. Then cut and serve.

PEANUT BUTTER SPRINKLE: Spread one baked brownie with creamy or chunky peanut butter. Then top with chocolate or rainbow sprinkles, flaked coconut, raisins, or granola. Eat.

CHOCOLATE CHIP BLONDIES

Even if you love chocolate, you can fall in love with these blondies. They're chewy with a strong taste of butterscotch (from the brown sugar). And they're filled with chocolate chips. The chips blend with the very soft middle to give you a mouthful of chocolate when you take a bite. You make them the same way you make the brownies in this chapter. And like the brownies, you only need a saucepan to mix the batter— no extra bowls.

What You Need

large saucepan

potholder

mixing spoon

8″ square baking pan

aluminum foil, if you want to line the pan (see A Baker's Trick, page 30)

cake tester or toothpick

cooling rack

measuring cups and spoons

shortening or vegetable shortening spray to grease pan

1 stick (4 ounces) salted butter

1 cup brown sugar

1 teaspoon vanilla extract

2 large or extra-large eggs

1¼ cups all-purpose flour

1 cup (6 ounces) semisweet chocolate chips

What You Do

1. Set out all your ingredients and equipment.

2. Grease an 8″ square baking pan. (Line it with foil first, if you like.) Preheat oven to 375 degrees. (If you use a glass pan, preheat the oven to 350 degrees.)

3. Put butter into saucepan over low heat. Use potholder to hold handle of pan and swirl pan every now and then until butter melts. Remove from heat.

4. Add brown sugar and stir to blend.

5. Add vanilla extract and stir.

6. Add eggs, one at a time, and stir to blend.

7. Add flour and stir gently but well. You want to blend all the flour in without beating in any air.

8. Stir in chocolate chips.

9. Spread batter in pan. Use the spatula to scrape the pan. Smooth the top of the batter.

10. Place pan in preheated oven. Bake 25 to 30 minutes. After 25 minutes, use a cake tester or toothpick to check for doneness (see Handy Helpers, page 93). Use potholder to remove pan from oven.

11. Cool on rack about 30 minutes.

12. Remove blondies from pan and cool completely. Cut into bars.

Makes approximately 16 large or 32 small blondies.

KITCHEN SINK BARS

These bar cookies have a little of everything thrown into them—everything but the kitchen sink! And you won't fill the kitchen sink with dishes when you make them. Just layer each ingredient into your baking pan. If you can sprinkle and pour, you can make these.

What You Need

9″ × 13″ inch baking pan

rubber spatula or spoon

potholder

cooling rack

measuring spoon

½ cup (4 ounces) butter or margarine, unsalted if possible

1½ cups graham cracker crumbs (about 11 crackers' worth)

1 teaspoon cinnamon

1 can (14 ounces) sweetened condensed milk (not evaporated milk)

1 cup (6 ounces) semisweet chocolate chips

½ cup raisins

½ cup chopped nuts

½ cup rolled oats or quick oats (not instant)

44

What You Do

1. Set out all your ingredients and equipment.

2. Preheat oven to 350 degrees. (If you use a glass pan, pre-heat the oven to 325 degrees.)

3. Place butter or margarine in baking pan and place in pre-heating oven until butter or margarine is melted, about 2 or 3 minutes.

4. Use a potholder to remove pan every minute or so to check that butter or margarine doesn't burn.

5. Set pan on cooling rack.

6. Spread graham cracker crumbs over melted butter or margarine. Pat crumbs gently to make an even layer, but don't burn your fingers.

7. Sprinkle cinnamon over crumbs.

8. Pour sweetened condensed milk evenly over cinnamon and crumbs. Use spatula to scrape milk out of can.

9. Sprinkle chocolate chips over milk.

10. Sprinkle raisins over chocolate chips.

11. Sprinkle nuts over raisins.

12. Sprinkle oats over nuts.

13. Place pan in oven. Bake 25 to 30 minutes, until oats and nuts begin to turn light brown.

14. Remove from oven and cool completely. Cut into bars. Store loosely covered at room temperature.

Makes 32 large bars.

COCONUT SHORTBREAD BARS

T hese cookies are made in three layers: The base is baked shortbread. Chocolate chips and coconut are then sprinkled on top. The cookies are crunchy and chewy.

What You Need

large mixing bowl

spoon

measuring cups and spoons

cooling rack

8″ square baking pan

aluminum foil, if you want to line the pan (see A Baker's Trick, page 30)

potholder

cooling rack

knife or spatula for spreading

shortening or vegetable shortening spray to grease pan

½ cup butter or margarine, at room temperature

½ cup sugar

1 cup all-purpose flour

1 cup (6 ounces) semisweet chocolate chips

½ cup shredded or flaked coconut

What You Do

1. Set out all your ingredients and equipment.

2. Preheat oven to 350 degrees. (If you use a glass pan, pre-heat the oven to 325 degrees.)

3. Grease pan or line it with foil first and grease the foil.

4. Beat butter or margarine with a spoon until it is very soft and creamy. (If it is room temperature, it should be very easy to stir.)

5. Add sugar and beat until mixture is all one color. You shouldn't be able to see any lumps of shortening or bits of sugar on the side of the bowl.

6. Add flour and stir to mix completely. The batter will be stiff. Just keep stirring until all the flour is mixed in. The mixture will be crumbly.

7. Pour or spoon the mixture into the greased pan. Pat and press the crumbs down into an even layer. The surface doesn't have to be completely smooth, but try to make it even all around.

8. Bake shortbread base about 24 minutes. When the top of the shortbread is just beginning to turn golden brown, use a potholder to take the pan from the oven. Set the pan on a cooling rack or other surface that will not burn.

9. Begin sprinkling chocolate chips all around the edge of the shortbread. (Be careful not to touch the hot pan as you work.) Then fill in the center of the pan with chips.

10. Put the pan back in the oven for 2 more minutes. Remove the pan and put it on the cooling rack again.

11. Use a knife or spatula to spread the melted chocolate chips across the cake.

12. Sprinkle the coconut evenly over the melted chocolate. Press the coconut lightly into the chocolate. (Don't burn your fingers.)

13. Cool completely. You can refrigerate for a while to set the chocolate more quickly.

14. Cut into bars (the base will be hard, so ask for help, if you need it). Serve at room temperature.

Makes approximately 16 large bars.

Everyone knows chocolate is fattening, but is it only sugar and calories? Absolutely not! A 1½ ounce milk chocolate bar with peanuts has more protein than an apple or a small box of raisins. Chocolate bars are also high in calcium.

And here's more good news. There is no truth to the idea that chocolate causes acne or pimples.

PEANUT BUTTER BROWNIES

 hese brownies are soft, chewy peanut butter cake with melted chocolate chips on top.

What You Need

large mixing bowl

spoon

measuring cups and spoons

9″ square baking pan

aluminum foil, if you want to line the pan (see A Baker's Trick, page 30)

potholder

cooling rack

knife and spatula

shortening or vegetable shortening spray to grease pan

2 tablespoons butter or margarine, at room temperature

½ cup creamy peanut butter

1½ cups sugar

2 eggs

1¼ cups flour

¼ teaspoon salt

1 cup (6 ounces) semisweet chocolate chips

What You Do

1. Set out all your ingredients and equipment.

2. Preheat oven to 350 degrees. (If you use a glass pan, preheat the oven to 325 degrees.)

3. Grease a 9″ square pan, or line it with foil first and then grease it.

4. In a large mixing bowl, stir together butter or margarine and peanut butter until they are well blended.

5. Stir in sugar.

6. Add eggs, one at a time, and stir well.

7. Add the vanilla and stir.

8. Add flour and salt and stir. The batter will be very stiff. Don't give up. Just keep stirring until all the flour is mixed in.

9. Put the batter into the greased pan. It will be too stiff to pour. Use a spoon or dump the batter from the bowl into the pan. Press the batter with your knuckles or fingertips to spread the batter. It doesn't have to be smooth. Just try to make a fairly even layer.

10. Bake for 18 minutes. When the top of the brownies is just beginning to turn golden, use a potholder to take the pan from the oven. Set it on a cooling rack or other surface that won't burn.

11. Sprinkle the chocolate chips over the top of the brownies. Be careful not to burn yourself as you work. Begin by sprinkling chips all around the edge of the pan. Then fill in the center of the pan with chips.

12. Put the pan back in the oven for 2 minutes.

13. Remove the pan to the cooling rack again.

14. Use a knife or spatula to spread the melted chocolate chips across the brownies. Use a knife to draw lines in the melted chocolate where you will cut the brownies into bars later on.

15. Let the brownies cool completely. (You can chill them to make the chocolate set faster.) Cut into bars and serve.

Makes approximately 16 large or 32 small bars.

CHOCO-FACTS

- **The average American eats 10 pounds of chocolate a year! That's a lot, but get this . . .**

- **The average person in Switzerland eats 22 pounds of chocolate a year! That's the world's record.**

5 DELIGHTFUL DESSERTS

This is a chapter of special desserts. Of course, some people would say that *anything* made with chocolate is special. (And others would say that anything made *without* chocolate isn't dessert.) But these desserts are for the big occasions. A birthday or a baseball or soccer game. The last day of school. Or anytime you want to celebrate BIG.

SPECIAL NOTE: Many of the recipes in this chapter are coded with three chocolate chips. Make sure an adult is nearby to help you make these special treats.

CHOCOLATE MOUSSE

Chocolate mousse is a cross between chocolate pudding and chocolate whipped cream. *Mousse* is pronounced like "moose." It is a French word that means "froth" or "foam." Like froth or foam, a mousse should be light and airy. This one is light and airy *and* chocolatey. If you want to be fancy, call it by its full French name: Say MOOSE oh SHAW-co-LA (*mousse au chocolat*).

A mousse is an elegant dessert, but it's not hard to make. You just have to learn to fold. Folding in cooking isn't like folding sheets. To fold you have to work gently. Think light, light, light. Then follow the directions.

What You Need

mixing bowls and hot water
    for melting chocolate (see Basics, pages
    6–7)

medium mixing bowl

large mixing bowl

electric mixer

rubber spatula

measuring cups and spoons

large serving bowl or 6 glasses or small
    bowls

1 cup (6 ounces) semisweet chocolate chips

2 eggs, at room temperature

1 tablespoon sugar

1 cup very cold heavy or whipping cream

1 teaspoon vanilla extract

53

What You Do

1. Set out all your ingredients and equipment.

2. Place the medium mixing bowl in the refrigerator (or in the freezer if there's room) to chill.

3. Melt the chocolate chips over hot water (see Basics, pages 6–7).

4. In the large mixing bowl, beat the eggs with the electric beater. Start with the beater on low and then turn it up until it is on high. When eggs begin to get foamy, sprinkle in the tablespoon of sugar. Keep beating (about 3 minutes) until the eggs are thick and very light in color.

5. Use the spatula to scrape the chocolate into the beaten eggs.

6. Use the electric mixer on low to blend the chocolate and eggs. Beat just until they are blended. Don't wash the mixer blades.

7. Pour the cream into the chilled mixing bowl. Add the vanilla extract.

8. Beat the cream on high until it is very thick. It should begin to show sharp ridges from the mixer and look peaked when you lift the beater. (But don't keep beating it or it will begin to turn to butter and you won't be able to use it.)

9. Remove the mixer and scrape the cream from the blades.

10. *Now you're ready to fold:* Add about one quarter of the whipped cream to the chocolate mixture. Use the rubber spatula to lightly stir the cream into the mixture. You want to lighten the chocolate mixture without beating all the air out of the whipped cream.

11. Add about half of the rest of the whipped cream to the bowl.

12. Use the rubber spatula to *fold* the cream into the batter. To do this, place the spatula against the inside of the bowl. Bring the spatula gently down under the chocolate mixture. Pull it across the bottom of the bowl. Then as you bring it back up to the surface, fold some of the batter up and over the whipped cream that's lying on top of the batter.

13. Give the bowl a quarter turn (as if the bowl were a steering wheel and you were turning a little to the right) and repeat the steps with the spatula.

14. Keep folding the batter gently over the whipped cream and turning the bowl until the cream and the batter are blended and there are no streaks of white. That's folding!

15. Pour the mousse into a serving bowl or into six glasses or dessert bowls.

16. Chill at least three hours before serving. If you want to keep the mousse longer than that, cover with plastic wrap.

Here's a tip. Chocolate is a very attractive food. That doesn't mean it's pretty. It means that chocolate picks up odors from other food. So it's always a good idea to keep chocolate wrapped up tightly—otherwise your chocolate might end up tasting like tuna fish. Hmmmm ... tuna fish chocolate. That might not be bad.

GRASSHOPPER-IN-THE-MUD PIE
🍫🍫🍫

Of you want to impress your family and friends, this bug will do it! It's a cross between two kinds of pie: a grasshopper pie (mint cream in a cookie crust) and a Mississippi mud pie (ice cream in a cookie crust with chocolate on top). This pie tastes like some of each. It has a mint cookie crust, a frozen chocolate-mint filling, and a chocolate-mint topping.

The filling is made the same way as the chocolate mousse on pages 53–55, so check those ingredients and equipment before you begin.

There are three steps to making this pie: the crust, the filling, and the topping. It's a lot of work, but it's worth it.

What You Need

9″ pie plate

large mixing bowl

FOR THE PIE CRUST: 28 chocolate sandwich cookies with mint filling, made into crumbs *(see note at end of recipe)*

4 tablespoons butter or margarine, melted

FOR THE FILLING: the same ingredients and equipment you see in the recipe on pages 53–55 for chocolate mousse, with these changes: instead of 1 cup semisweet chocolate chips, use 1 cup mint chocolate chips *(see note at end of recipe).* You don't add any vanilla extract, and you don't need a serving bowl or a sheet of plastic wrap

56

FOR THE TOPPING: mixing bowls and hot water for melting chocolate (see Basics, pages 6–7)

1 cup (5 ounces) mint chocolate chips *(see note at end of recipe)*

2 tablespoons butter or margarine, unsalted if possible

What You Do

MAKE THE PIE CRUST:

1. Set out all your ingredients and equipment.

2. Make sure there is room in your freezer for a 9″ pie plate to sit flat with nothing on top of it.

3. Place cookie crumbs and melted butter or margarine in large mixing bowl.

4. Mix well with a fork.

5. Pour crumbs into a pie plate.

6. Use a spoon to press the crumbs into place along the bottom and make a wall of crumbs around the side. Press very gently at first. Try to make an even layer about ½″ thick all around. The crumbs should come up to the top of the pie plate along the sides. When crumbs are evenly spread, press a little harder to make a solid layer of crumbs.

7. Freeze crust while you make the filling.

MAKE THE FILLING:

1. Follow the recipe for making chocolate mousse on page 53.

2. When you finish the mousse, pour it into the frozen cookie crust and place it in the freezer.

3. After about one hour, place a sheet of plastic wrap over the pie and continue to freeze at least five more hours or overnight.

MAKE THE TOPPING:

1. Melt chocolate over hot water (see Basics, pages 6–7).

2. Add butter or margarine and stir until smooth.

3. Remove frozen pie from freezer.

4. Uncover and spread melted chocolate mixture evenly over top. Work quickly to cover pie before chocolate hardens.

5. Place pie back in freezer for five minutes and then serve. Or cover pie with plastic wrap and freeze until ready to serve.

6. Ask an adult for help in cutting the pie. Use the point of a sharp knife to cut a line in the chocolate topping. Then cut down through the line into the mousse filling. Then cut through the cookie crust. The crust will be thick and hard. It may take some strength to cut through it. When the first cut is through to the pie plate, repeat to make a second cut.

SPECIAL NOTE: If you can't find mint cookies, use regular ones. If you can't find mint chocolate chips, you can use semi-sweet chocolate chips and add ¼ teaspoon of peppermint extract to the mousse mixture and 2 or 3 drops of peppermint extract to the chocolate topping. If you don't like mint, use regular cookies and regular chocolate chips and don't leave out the vanilla extract in the mousse recipe.

MINI CHOCOLATE CHEESECAKES

Some people get crazy about cheesecake. For them, it is *the* dessert. The *only* dessert. So what if you add chocolate to cheesecake? You make *the* dessert better—*much* better!

What You Need

mixing bowls and hot water for melting chocolate (see Basics, page 6–7)

small and large mixing bowls

rubber spatula

fork

mixing spoon

tablespoon

12-hole muffin tin (opening should measure about 1½" across)

12 paper-lined foil cupcake liners *or* 24 paper cupcake liners (use 2 paper liners for each)

cooling rack

measuring cups and spoons

FOR CRUST: slightly less than 1 cup graham cracker crumbs (7 whole graham crackers)

3 tablespoons sugar

3 tablespoons butter or margarine, melted

FOR CHEESECAKE: 1 cup (6 ounces) semi-sweet chocolate chips

1 tablespoon butter or margarine, at room temperature

8 ounces (large package) cream cheese, at room temperature

⅓ cup sugar

2 eggs, at room temperature

1 cup (8-ounce container) vanilla yogurt

1 teaspoon vanilla extract

What You Do:

MAKE CRUST:

1. Set out all your ingredients and equipment.

2. In a small bowl, mix together graham cracker crumbs and sugar. Stir in melted butter or margarine and use a fork to mix well.

3. Place paper-lined foil cupcake liners in openings in muffin tin. (Or put two paper ones together into each opening.)

4. Spoon a heaping tablespoon of crumb mixture into each cupcake liner. Divide any leftover crumbs evenly among cups.

5. Use your thumb to press crumbs into bottom and about ½ inch up the side of each muffin cup. The crusts don't have to be too neat, but be sure the bottom of each cup has a layer of packed crumbs.

MAKE CHEESECAKE MIXTURE:

1. Preheat oven to 350 degrees.

2. Melt chocolate chips over hot water (see Basics, page 6–7). When chocolate is melted, add the tablespoon of soft butter to bowl and stir to blend.

3. In large mixing bowl, beat cream cheese with sugar until well blended.

4. Add eggs and beat to blend.

5. Add melted chocolate and blend well. Stir in yogurt and then vanilla and blend.

6. Pour about ¼ cup cheesecake mixture over crumbs in each cupcake liner. Divide any leftover mixture among cups.

7. Place in preheated oven and bake 22 to 26 minutes. The cheesecakes are ready when the tops no longer look wet in the middle. The filling will puff up in the oven. They will settle back down as the cakes cool.

8. Use a potholder to remove muffin tray from oven and cool on cooling rack. Then refrigerate at least one hour.

9. To remove cheesecakes from muffin tin, pull gently on the paper or foil muffin cup liner. If you have trouble getting the cakes out, dip the bottom of the muffin tray in hot water for a few seconds. Then tug again at the cup liners. Keep cheesecakes covered in the refrigerator until ready to serve.

Makes 12.

FUDGE-NUT PIE

Pecan pie is a special dessert from the American South. This recipe makes a dessert that's part pecan pie, part fudge pie. And since chocolate goes well with walnuts *or* pecans, you can use either nut to make this. (If you use walnuts, you get a flavor that may remind you of brownies—unless you eat a lot of pecan brownies.)

What You Need

large saucepan and potholder

rubber spatula

baking sheet large enough to catch drips from 8" pie pan

measuring cups and spoons

unbaked 8" pie crust (you can buy one frozen)

¾ cup walnuts or pecans (use halves or smaller pieces)

3 tablespoons butter or margarine

¾ cup semisweet chocolate chips

½ cup brown sugar

3 eggs

½ cup corn syrup

½ teaspoon vanilla extract

What You Do

1. Set out all your ingredients and equipment.

2. Preheat oven to 350 degrees.

3. Remove pie crust from freezer. If there is paper lining in the crust, remove the paper.

4. Spread the nut pieces across the bottom of the pie crust. Place pie crust on baking sheet. Set aside.

5. Place butter or margarine in large saucepan and melt over medium heat. Using a potholder to hold the handle, swirl the pan occasionally to keep the shortening from boiling.

6. Remove pan from heat and add chocolate chips.

7. Stir melted shortening and chips until mixture is smooth.

8. Add the brown sugar and stir to blend. Don't worry if there are small lumps of sugar.

9. Add one egg and blend gently until no white or yolk is showing. Don't beat too hard. You don't want to beat air into the batter. Add second and third eggs the same way.

10. Stir in corn syrup and vanilla extract.

11. Pour batter over nuts in pie crust.

12. Put baking sheet with filled crust in preheated oven. Bake 55 to 60 minutes.

13. Check to see if the pie is ready after 50 minutes. To do this use a potholder and gently shake the baking sheet to see if the filling is still liquid in the center. If it jiggles, the pie is not ready. Filling will puff up, first around the edges and then in the center. (The filling will settle back down as the pie cools.)

14. Carefully remove the baking sheet from the oven when the pie is done and allow the pie to cool completely before cutting into it. If you like, serve this pie with whipped cream or vanilla ice cream.

Serves 6 to 8.

CLOUD NINES

🍫🍫🍫

This is a recipe for very patient cooks. It's a chocolate cup filled with cocoa whipped cream and topped with sprinkles or nuts.

Making the chocolate cups is what takes patience. It might take several tries to get it right. But if you like to use your hands and you like chocolate, this recipe is for you. You need paper drinking cups to make this dessert. They have to be the wax-covered paper type—not plain paper and not plastic.

What You Need

mixing bowls and hot water for melting chocolate
(see Basics, pages 6–7)

tablespoon

scissors

cellophane tape

small spoon or small knife

6 or 8 paper cups (kitchen dispenser size, 2¾" high)

medium mixing bowl

mixer

measuring cups

FOR CHOCOLATE CUPS: 1 cup (6 ounces)
semisweet chocolate chips

FOR COCOA CREAM: 1 cup heavy or whipping cream

½ **cup confectioners' sugar**

¼ **cup cocoa powder**

nuts or sprinkles

What You Do

MAKE CHOCOLATE CUPS:

1. Set out all your ingredients and equipment. (Leave cream in refrigerator.) Place medium mixing bowl and mixer blades in freezer while you make the chocolate cups.

2. Melt chocolate chips over hot water (see Basics, page 4).

3. Use scissors to slit one paper cup from its rim down to the bottom. Do *not* cut into the bottom of the cup! Use two pieces of cellophane tape to tape across the slit. The cup should look as if you haven't cut it. Don't worry, though, if the whole slit isn't sealed.

4. Make up 3 more cups the same way. Save the other cups in case you have to redo any of the chocolate cups later.

5. Place 2 heaping tablespoonfuls of melted chocolate into one of the prepared paper cups. Use the handle of the small spoon or the blade of the small knife to smooth the chocolate around the inside of the paper cup. Bring the chocolate up the sides of the cup, all the way to the rim. Don't go over the rim. Try to make an even layer of chocolate around the inside of the cup. Don't worry if the chocolate is thicker toward the bottom, but don't make it thinner than $\frac{1}{8}''$ around the top. Hold the chocolate-filled cup up to the light to see if there are any bare spots in the walls of chocolate. (The light will show through if the chocolate is too thin.)

6. Place the cup in the freezer for about 30 minutes or in the refrigerator for 60 minutes. Fill the other 3 cups the same way and chill them, too.

7. When the cups are chilled, you are ready to take the paper off. You will have to work quickly and carefully. Begin by rinsing your hands in very cold water. Dry your hands. Take one chocolate cup out of freezer or refrigerator. Peel off the pieces of tape. Very carefully peel back the paper cup from the wall of chocolate. Peel down from the rim along the slit. When you get to the bottom, gently tear the paper cup so that you leave the bottom of the cup attached to the chocolate. Tear all the way around the bottom of the cup so that you remove the sides. When you have only the bottom left, carefully pull off the paper circle and set the chocolate cup on a plate or tray and put it in the refrigerator. Repeat with the other cups.

One thing might go wrong: The chocolate might crack as you take the paper off. If that happens, put the chocolate back in the bowl and melt it again and make a new cup. When the 4 cups are finished, they are ready to be filled with cocoa cream.

MAKE COCOA CREAM:

1. Pour cream into chilled mixing bowl.

2. Add confectioners' sugar and cocoa.

3. When you first begin to whip the cream, the cocoa, sugar, and cream will no doubt splatter, so clear the area where you are working. Begin beating with chilled blades on low speed until well blended.

4. Raise the speed to medium and then to high and beat until cream is thick. It should leave points when you lift the mixer blade out of the cream. (Turn off the mixer before testing for the points, or you'll spray the cream all over the kitchen.)

5. Spoon one fourth of the whipped cream into each of the chocolate cups. Cover the top with sprinkles or chopped nuts and refrigerate until you are ready to serve.

Makes 4 Cloud Nines.

S'MORE PUDDING

Almost everybody knows about s'mores. To make a s'more, you toast a marshmallow over a campfire. Then you put it on a graham cracker, cover it with a piece of milk chocolate and another graham cracker. What do you get? A warm, gooey sandwich of marshmallow and melting chocolate that tastes so good, you want s'more!

This pudding has all the flavor of a s'more without the campfire. It's a creamy mixture of chocolate and marshmallow with chunks of graham cracker stirred in.

What You Need

large saucepan

rubber spatula

measuring cups

serving bowl

1 cup milk

15 regular-size marshmallows

1 cup (about 6 ounces) milk chocolate chips
(or you can use 6 ounces of any other milk
chocolate; break or cut it into small pieces)

4 whole graham crackers, crumbled into
small pieces

What You Do

1. Set out all your ingredients and equipment.

2. Pour milk into saucepan.

3. Add marshmallows and set over low heat. Stir occasionally until marshmallows begin to melt and mixture becomes foamy. Then keep stirring so mixture does not stick. When mixture is smooth and all marshmallows are melted, remove from heat.

4. Stir in chocolate until it is melted and mixture is smooth. Allow mixture to cool to room temperature.

5. Stir in broken graham crackers and pour into serving bowl. Refrigerate at least 2 hours.

Makes 4 servings.

It's hard to imagine a world without chocolate chips—but they've only been around for about 50 years. In 1930 a woman named Ruth Wakefield came up with the idea—by accident! She cut a chocolate bar into little pieces and stirred the chocolate chunks into her cookie batter. She figured the chocolate would melt and make the batter better. To her amazement, the chips stayed whole and the chocolate chip cookie was born! Chip Chip Hooray!

CHOCOLATE LAYER CAKE

You never know when you'll need a chocolate cake. It could be someone's birthday, an anniversary, or just a rainy day. Whatever the reason, you can make this cake in a hurry. Once you get the ingredients lined up, you just add them to a big bowl and stir.

Frost the tops and sides of these layers with Chocolate Fudge Frosting (see page 36). You'll need to double the ingredients for the frosting recipe.

What You Need

large mixing bowl

wire whisk or large spoon

measuring cups and spoons

rubber spatula

two 9" round baking pans

potholder

three cooling racks—or one cooling rack, two sheets of wax paper, and a plate large enough to cover a baking pan

shortening (don't use vegetable shortening spray) and some extra flour for greasing and flouring the pans

3 cups flour

2½ cups sugar

½ cup cocoa powder

½ teaspoon salt

2 teaspoons baking soda

2 tablespoons vinegar

1 tablespoon vanilla extract

1 cup vegetable (but not olive) oil

2 cups cold water

What You Do

1. Set out all your ingredients and equipment.

2. Preheat oven to 350 degrees.

3. Grease the baking pans.

4. Add about a tablespoon of flour to one of the pans. Gently shake and pat the side of the pan to spread the flour all over the bottom. (Add a bit more flour if you are running out.)

5. Next, hold the pan over the sink or trash can and tilt the pan so that the flour moves along the side of the pan and sticks to the grease. Turn the pan slowly so that the flour moves along the entire side of the pan.

6. The inside of the pan should now be coated with flour. Tap any extra flour left in the pan into the second pan. Add a bit more flour to the second pan and cover the inside with flour as you did with the first pan. Tap any extra flour from the second pan into the trash or sink.

7. Put 3 cups flour, the sugar, cocoa powder, salt, and baking soda into a large mixing bowl. Use a whisk or spoon to stir until everything is well blended and there are no lumps of cocoa left.

8. Use the spoon or whisk to pat down the center of the dry ingredients.

9. Pour the vinegar, vanilla, oil, and water into the center of the dry ingredients.

10. Stir everything together until the batter is well mixed and there are no lumps.

11. Divide the batter between the two pans. Fill each pan about $1/3$ full and then add a little more batter to each until they are evenly filled.

12. Use a rubber spatula to scrape out any batter that sticks to the bowl.

13. Bake cake layers in preheated oven about 40 to 45 minutes. After 40 minutes, test for doneness using a cake tester.

14. Use potholders to remove layers from oven. Place on cooling rack and cool 15 minutes in pans.

15. If you have three cooling racks, put one rack over the top of one layer. (Or if you don't have three cooling racks, put a sheet of wax paper over the top and then put a plate over the wax paper. The top of the plate should face the top of the cake.)

16. Use a potholder to hold the pan with one hand while you hold the cooling rack or plate with the other. Carefully turn the pan and the rack or plate over so that the cake is resting on the rack or plate. Set the rack or plate down.

17. Gently lift the pan and let the cake slip out. (If any of the cake is stuck to the pan, loosen it with a knife and set the piece in place on the cake, like you would put a piece in a jigsaw puzzle.)

18. Take a cooling rack and place it over the cake. The rack will be resting on the bottom of the cake. Lift the rack or plate that the cake is resting on in one hand and put your other hand over the cooling rack that is on top of the cake. The cake will be between the two.

19. Turn them all over carefully so that the cake is sitting right side up on a cooling rack. Lift off the plate or rack that is now on top of the cake and let the cake cool completely. (While the cake cools, make the frosting.)

20. If one of the layers is thicker, let that one be the bottom. Turn the bottom layer upside down onto a large plate. Spread frosting on the layer. Go almost to the edge of the layer. Don't frost the sides yet. (If you like, sprinkle ½ cup of miniature marshmallows or chopped nuts or miniature chocolate chips on top of the frosting between the layers. Pat them down into the frosting.)

21. Gently place the bottom of the second layer over the frosting and line them up so that they are even.

22. Spread frosting all around the sides of the two layers. Make sure the frosting covers the whole side and goes all the way up to the top of the cake.

23. Frost the top of the cake.

Makes 8 servings.

CHOCOLATE PARTIES

Do you have a special occasion coming up? Why not make it a chocolate celebration? The parties in this chapter are made for chocolate lovers and their friends.

CHOCOLATE FONDUE PARTY

Imagine swimming in a big vat of warm melted chocolate. You've just pictured a giant fondue. *Fondue* is a French word that means "melted." The most well-known fondue is made with melted cheese and is eaten as a meal. But this chocolate fondue is meant strictly for dessert. And though it's not big enough to swim in, it's perfect for taking a dip.

What You Need

a large saucepan and a shallow dish large enough to hold the pan or fondue pot and burner

plastic or wooden-handled spoon

long thin dipping forks or regular forks

paper plates

napkins

a large plate or platter

bite-size pieces of fruit, such as banana chunks, apple slices, orange sections, pineapple chunks, pear slices, strawberries, and chunks of pound cake or bread

4 tablespoons butter

½ cup milk

3 tablespoons sugar

2 cups (12 ounces) chocolate chips

What You Do

1. Set out all your ingredients and equipment.

2. Put fruit, cake, or bread pieces on large plate. Set out forks, plates, and napkins.

3. Mix butter, milk, and sugar in saucepan or fondue pot and heat over low heat until butter melts. Stir to blend.

4. Remove pot from heat and add chocolate, stirring to help melt chocolate evenly. If mixture gets too cool, place it over very low heat for a few seconds and keep stirring.

5. When chocolate melts and mixture is smooth, fondue is ready. If you have a fondue set, place the pot over a low flame to keep the chocolate warm. If you are using a saucepan, place it in a pan of hot water and change the water if it gets too cool.

6. Set fondue in a place that is within reach of the party guests. Use the forks to spear pieces of fruit, bread, or cake and dip them in the melted chocolate. Enjoy.

SPECIAL NOTE: If you don't have time to melt chocolate for an authentic fondue, you can use any chocolate syrup. Just pour the syrup into a bowl, spear a favorite goodie, and dip!

MAKE-YOUR-OWN
SUNDAE PARTY

Anyone can make a chocolate ice-cream sundae. But it takes a real expert to make *the most chocolatey* chocolate ice-cream sundae. Why not have a sundae contest at your next party? Begin with plenty of chocolate ice cream. (You can also use vanilla or another flavor if you want to.) Then line up dishes of chocolate things to scatter on top: broken-up chocolate bars, chocolate sprinkles, chocolate chips, M&M's®, chocolate cookie chunks. You can also use a few non-chocolate toppers: frozen or fresh berries, sliced bananas, granola, nuts, miniature marshmallows. Top it all off with a Heavenly Chocolate Sauce and dig in.

HEAVENLY SAUCE #1 THICK AND SMOOTH FUDGE SAUCE

If you like your fudge hot and thick, this sauce is for you.

What You Need

small saucepan

wooden spoon or a plastic-handled metal
  spoon

potholder

measuring cups and spoons

½ cup corn syrup

1 cup (6 ounces) semisweet chocolate chips

1 teaspoon vanilla extract

2 tablespoons butter or margarine

3 tablespoons heavy or whipping cream or
evaporated milk or whole milk

What You Do

1. Set out all your ingredients and equipment.

2. Put corn syrup and chocolate chips in saucepan over very
low heat.

3. Use potholder to hold pan by the handle. Stir constantly as
you melt the chocolate chips and blend them with the corn
syrup. Leave the pan on the heat for only 4 or 5 seconds at a
time. Then lift it off for about 5 seconds. Keep heating and lifting the pan as you continue to stir.

4. When the chocolate is melted and blended with the corn
syrup, take the pan off the heat.

5. Add the vanilla extract and the butter or margarine. Stir to
blend. If necessary, put the pan back on the heat for a few
seconds to melt the shortening. Keep stirring.

6. When the mixture is smooth, stir in the cream or milk.

7. Use immediately, or store in a covered jar in the refrigerator.
This sauce can be used warm or at room temperature. When
it is cold, it is too thick to use.

8. To rewarm the sauce, place the jar in a bowl of hot water and
stir until it is evenly warm.

HEAVENLY SAUCE #2 CHOCOLATE-MARSHMALLOW SAUCE

If you like chocolate sauce and marshmallow cream, this is the sauce for you. It's thick and really sticks to your ice cream. It's even better with a sprinkling of nuts.

What You Need

small saucepan with cover

rubber spatula

measuring cups

½ cup heavy or whipping cream

1⅓ cups (about 8 ounces) milk chocolate chips

½ cup marshmallow cream

What You Do

1. Set out all your ingredients and equipment.

2. Pour cream into saucepan over medium heat.

3. Stir with rubber spatula and heat until cream just begins to simmer. Remove from heat. Stir in chocolate chips. Cover pan and let it sit a few minutes.

4. Then stir to blend. Add marshmallow cream and stir to blend well. Serve immediately over ice cream. If you aren't using the sauce right away, store it covered in the refrigerator. Before you use it, let it come to room temperature. Then place pan or jar in a bowl of boiling water to heat sauce gently.

HEAVENLY SAUCE #3 EASY COCOA SAUCE

This is a thin chocolate sauce with a lot going for it. It's not too hard to make. It tastes great. And you don't need a bunch of unusual ingredients to make it. There's a good chance you have everything you need in your kitchen right now.

You can use this as a syrup for drinks, too. If you do, just skip the last step—don't add the butter or margarine. And pour a bit of this sauce right into the nearest glass of milk.

What You Need

medium saucepan

spoon

potholder

measuring cups and spoons

1 cup sugar

1 cup water

½ cup cocoa powder

½ teaspoon vanilla extract

1 tablespoon plus 1 teaspoon butter or
  margarine

What You Do

1. Set out all your ingredients and equipment.

2. Put the sugar and water together in the saucepan. Set over medium heat. Stir occasionally until sugar dissolves completely. You won't see any sugar at all, only clear liquid. Stop stirring.

3. Bring the mixture to a full boil. Boil without stirring for four minutes. Remove from heat.

4. Add cocoa and stir until there are no lumps.

5. Stir in vanilla.

6. Cut butter or margarine into four pieces and add them to the mixture. Stir to blend as butter or margarine melts. Use warm sauce over ice cream, or allow the sauce to cool and store in refrigerator until needed. When you're ready to use it again, let it come to room temperature. Then to warm the sauce, place the jar carefully in a bowl of very hot water.

CHOCOLATE-FOR-BREAKFAST PARTY

This party idea is a real eye-opener. Chocolate goodies on the breakfast table! It's just the thing to energize your sleepy guests after a slumber party. Or get the jump on a birthday celebration with the first party of the day.

Breakfast ideas: hot chocolate or cocoa or banana smoothie (see pages 10–16); or the night before, put together a half recipe of chocolate fondue (see pages 75–76) and refrigerate it in a covered container overnight. Take it out a half hour before breakfast and use it as a rich, chocolatey spread for bread or toast. (Try it with peanut butter!)

COCOA FRENCH TOAST

Is French toast from France? Yes and no. When the French make French toast, they call it *pain perdu*, or "lost bread." You can also find Spanish toast, Portuguese toast, German toast, and Argentine toast. *This* recipe could come from the Land of Chocolate. If you serve it for dessert instead of for breakfast, try it with a scoop of vanilla ice cream.

What You Need

large mixing bowl

small bowl

mixing spoon

knife

pancake turner

8″ square baking pan

potholder

measuring cups and spoons

4 slices whole-wheat or white bread

shortening or vegetable cooking spray to
   grease pan

2 tablespoons unsweetened cocoa powder

¼ cup sugar

¼ cup milk

2 eggs

¼ teaspoon vanilla extract

2 dashes of cinnamon

What You Do

1. Set out all your ingredients and equipment.

2. Preheat oven to 350 degrees. (If you use a glass pan, preheat the oven to 325 degrees.)

3. Cut bread diagonally in quarters so you have four triangles
from each piece.

4. Grease baking pan.

5. Place bread into baking pan. If the four slices don't fit in
lying flat, it's okay to let some of the pieces stick up a bit.

6. Put the cocoa powder and the sugar into the bowl. Mix them well with the spoon to get rid of all the cocoa lumps.

7. Stir in the milk and mix well.

8. Add the eggs.

9. Beat the cocoa-egg mixture with a spoon until it is smooth.

10. Stir in vanilla extract and two dashes of cinnamon.

11. Pour the mixture over the bread in the baking pan. Let the bread soak up the mixture for about a minute. Pat down any part of the bread that is not soaking up the mixture. *Carefully* place the pan into the preheated oven.

12. After 15 minutes, use a potholder to remove the pan to see if the mixture is set. If any part of the bread still seems to be very wet, let it bake about 3 minutes longer. Remove from oven.

13. Remove the French toast from pan, using a pancake turner. If you like, serve with butter and maple syrup or honey.

Makes 4 servings.

Does money grow on trees? In the sixteenth century in Central America it did. Cocoa beans were used as money. People could buy a pumpkin for four cocoa beans.

COCOA-BANANA-OAT LOAF

This moist, sweet bread is perfect for breakfast. (Eat it plain or with cheese or butter.) It makes two loaves: one for breakfast and one for snacks or dessert. Try a slice topped with a scoop of ice cream.

What You Need

large mixing bowl

2 medium mixing bowls

potato masher or blender

wire whisk

mixing spoon

2 aluminum foil (disposable) loaf pans, 8″ × 4″

rubber spatula

potholder

cake tester or toothpick

cooling rack

measuring cups and spoons

shortening or vegetable shortening spray to
   grease pan

1 cup mashed ripe bananas (2½ small ones
   or 2 medium ones or 1½ large ones; measure after mashing)

2 eggs

1 cup brown sugar

½ cup vegetable oil

1 teaspoon vanilla extract

¾ cup white flour

½ cup whole-wheat flour

⅓ cup cocoa powder

1 teaspoon baking powder

1 teaspoon baking soda

1½ teaspoons cinnamon

¼ teaspoon salt

1 cup rolled or quick oats (not instant)

1 cup walnuts broken into small chunks

What You Do

1. Set out all your ingredients and equipment.

2. Preheat oven to 350 degrees.

3. Grease 2 loaf pans and set aside.

4. Peel bananas, break into halves or thirds, and put in a medium mixing bowl. Mash with potato masher (or grind bananas in blender.) Measure out 1 cup of banana. (Any leftover banana can be mixed into a glass of chocolate milk or a cup of yogurt.)

5. Break eggs into a large mixing bowl. Whisk lightly to break the yolks.

6. Add the brown sugar and whisk to mix. Mixture should be nearly smooth.

7. Add oil and mix well.

8. Stir in bananas and vanilla extract.

9. In a medium mixing bowl, place white flour, whole-wheat flour, cocoa powder, baking powder, baking soda, cinnamon, and salt.

10. Mix well with a wire whisk or spoon to break up the lumps in the cocoa.

11. Add flour mixture to large mixing bowl and stir lightly but well. Don't beat it hard.

12. When mixture is nearly smooth, add the oats and stir lightly but well.

13. Stir in the nuts.

14. Use a rubber spatula to scrape the batter into the greased loaf pans. Place pans in oven and bake 40 to 50 minutes. After 35 minutes, use cake tester or toothpick to test for doneness. Cool on rack about 30 minutes. Remove loaves from pan and finish cooling.

Makes 2 loaves.

CHOCOLATE CHIP PANCAKES

Ordinary pancakes turn into something very special when you add chocolate chips. Whole wheat pancakes are especially good.

What You Need

large mixing bowl

mixing spoon or wire whisk

measuring cups

griddle or frying pan

pancake turner

pancake batter (homemade or made from a mix)

chocolate chips or chopped chocolate

shortening for the griddle or skillet

What You Do

1. Before you begin, see if you have a ⅛ cup measure to use when you pour the batter onto the skillet or griddle. Two tablespoons is ⅛ cup. If you don't have a ⅛ cup measure, check to see if you have a large serving spoon that holds about 2 tablespoons of liquid. Use water to test it. Otherwise, you can use a ¼ cup measure but only fill it halfway.

2. Make up a batch of your favorite pancake batter. You can use a mix (buttermilk, whole wheat, or buckwheat) or make them from scratch. For every cup of flour or dry pancake mix you use, you will need ¼ cup chocolate chips— miniature chips work best in pancakes, or you can chop up your favorite chocolate bar.

3. Mix the batter. Don't mix it too hard. There should always be a few lumps left.

4. Stir in the chocolate chips.

5. Lightly grease and heat the griddle or skillet.

6. Pour a little less than 2 tablespoons of batter for each pancake.

7. When little bubbles appear all over the uncooked side of the pancake, it's time to turn it over.

8. Cook the second side until it's light brown. (You can peek underneath by lifting it with the pancake turner.) Remember that the first pancake doesn't usually come out perfectly, but the rest should be great.

You can serve these pancakes with maple syrup, but they are quite sweet even without syrup. Try plain or vanilla yogurt on top instead.

What in the world is white chocolate? Well, for starters, it isn't chocolate. It is sweetened cocoa butter. When cocoa is squeezed out of unsweetened chocolate paste, cocoa butter is left. Add milk and sugar and you've got white chocolate.

HANDY HELPERS

This section explains some of the ingredients, equipment, and cooking terms in this book. It also gives some inside tricks of the trade.

INGREDIENTS

BUTTER AND MARGARINE are types of *shortening.* All the recipes are made with salted shortening unless the recipe says *unsalted.* If you use unsalted shortening where it is not called for, add two dashes of salt to the recipe. (A dash is what you would get from one shake of a salt shaker.)

Most sticks of butter and margarine are marked with lines that show tablespoons and teaspoons.

one stick = 8 tablespoons
one stick = ½ cup
one stick = 4 ounces

CHOCOLATE There are many different types of chocolate. Some of the names can be confusing:

BAKING CHOCOLATE is unsweetened chocolate. It is also called *bitter chocolate.* If you roast cocoa beans and grind them, you get pure, unsweetened chocolate. Baking chocolate comes in paper-wrapped squares that are one ounce each.

SEMISWEET CHOCOLATE is bitter chocolate that has sugar, cocoa butter, and some other flavoring added to it. Semisweet chocolate chips are easy to measure, and the small pieces melt quickly. The chips come in bags that weigh 6 or 12 (or more) ounces. One cup of chocolate chips equals

6 ounces. You can use any type of semisweet or bittersweet chocolate for these recipes. If you use a chocolate bar, chop or break the bar into small pieces before you melt it.

MILK CHOCOLATE is sweetened chocolate with a special kind of dried milk added to it. You can now buy milk chocolate chips in many stores. Milk chocolate melts at a lower temperature than semisweet chocolate. It burns more easily, too.

COCOA POWDER is baking chocolate with the fat (cocoa butter) taken out. It has no sugar and no milk added to it. (You can buy sweetened cocoa mixes, but don't use them in a recipe calling for cocoa powder.)

To measure cocoa powder, spoon it loosely into a measuring cup. Don't pack it down. Hold the measuring cup over a bowl or container. Then level the top with a knife or spatula. If cocoa powder is too lumpy to measure, press it through a strainer into a bowl. Then spoon it into your measuring cup.

COOKIE CRUMBS To make crumbs from graham crackers, vanilla wafers, or sandwich cookies, you need a blender *or* a plastic bag, a twist tie, and a rolling pin.

If you use a blender: Break up the cookies and put them in the container. Blend until cookies are fine crumbs.

Or place cookies in a plastic bag. Close bag and seal with twist tie. Gently roll over cookies with rolling pin. Keep rolling over pieces until they are fine crumbs.

CORN SYRUP is a thick liquid sweetener made from corn. The recipes in this book use light or white corn syrup. To measure corn syrup, pour it into a measuring cup until it reaches the top. Use a spoon, spatula, or clean finger to scrape all the corn syrup out of the cup.

EGGS The eggs in these recipes should be *large* or *extra large*.

To make a *clean* break in an eggshell, give the egg a quick, not-too-hard rap against a counter edge or the edge of a mixing bowl. Then turn the egg and rap it again to spread the crack around the egg. Pry the crack open with your thumbs. If pieces of broken shell get mixed in with the egg, your food will have a crunch that you don't want. It's hard to grab a piece of eggshell once it slips into the bowl. But here's a trick: Use half an eggshell to scoop out the piece of shell.

Another trick: Before adding one or more eggs to a mixture, break one egg into a small bowl. Fish out any pieces of eggshell and then add the egg to the mixture. Break and add other eggs in the same way.

FLOUR The flour in these recipes is all-purpose white flour (unless the recipe says *whole wheat*). This flour is not the same as cake flour or self-rising flour.

Measure flour into a measuring cup by spooning it into the cup. Don't pack it down. Then hold the measuring cup over a bowl or container. Take a straight butter knife or a spatula and even the top. This *level* cup (or half cup or quarter cup, or whatever) is what you use in the recipe.

SUGAR All the sugar in these recipes is regular granulated white sugar, unless the recipe says something else. To measure sugar, dip the measuring cup into the sugar, or spoon the sugar into the cup. Use a knife or spatula to even the top. If a recipe calls for **brown sugar,** you can use light or dark. To measure brown sugar, pack the sugar into the measuring cup.

CONFECTIONERS' SUGAR is white sugar that is ground very fine. It is mixed with a little cornstarch. To measure confectioners' sugar, spoon it lightly into a measuring cup. Use a knife or spatula to even the top.

VANILLA EXTRACT is a flavoring that is made from a long black vanilla bean. You can also buy imitation vanilla flavor. It costs less but doesn't taste as good, especially when it is used in baked goods.

VEGETABLE SHORTENING SPRAY comes in a can that you can use to grease a pan. You give the pan (or the foil, if you line the pan) a very light coating of the spray.

EQUIPMENT

CAKE TESTER is a long, thin metal pick that you stick into the center of a cake to test if it is done. If the pick comes out clean, without bits of batter or crumbs sticking to it, the cake is ready. You can use a toothpick instead.

COOLING RACK is a wire rack on which you can safely set baked goods to cool. The rack is raised a little to let air flow under it. If you have no cooling rack, use a trivet or other surface that will not burn if you rest a hot pan on it.

RUBBER SPATULA is a rubber paddle on the end of a plastic or wooden handle. Use it to mix, stir, and to scrape batter or melted chocolate out of a bowl or measuring cup.

WIRE WHISK is made of wires which are bent into a curved light-bulb shape at the top and are joined together in a thin handle. A whisk is used to stir, beat, and whip things. It is good for getting lumps out of batter or beating air into mixtures.

COOKING TERMS

BOIL Bubbles show up all over the surface of a heated liquid. A rolling boil is when the bubbles really move.

SIMMER Tiny bubbles begin to appear around the edge of a heated liquid.

LOW, MEDIUM, OR HIGH HEAT On a gas stove, low heat is when the flame is very small. If you turned it any lower it would go off. A high flame flattens out along the bottom of the pan. It may even start to go up the sides of the pan. Medium is between the two. (If you use an electric stove, the numbers tell you which degree of heat you are using.)

OVEN TEMPERATURE Most ovens have a dial that lets you set the temperature you want the oven to be. Some ovens run hotter or cooler than the temperature dial says. When you ask permission to use the oven, ask if the temperature dial is right. You may have to set the oven 25 or 50 degrees hotter or colder than the dial says. If you have an oven thermometer, check to see if the oven is preheated to the right temperature. (Don't touch the thermometer. It gets hot when it sits in a hot oven. Read it *while* it is in the oven.)

INDEX